ANTIQUE
CUT GLASS

Consignment
Shop
Antiques

ANTIQUES
AND
COLLECTIBLES
SHOW
AND
SALE
JOURNAL
2
1
VULCAN
SALE
WILL JENKINS

NEW COMPANION
ESTATE SALE
ANTIQUES

E.A.P.
PARIS, FRANCE
ANTIQUES SHOW & SALE
MAPPIN & WEBB

VINTAGE JEWELRY

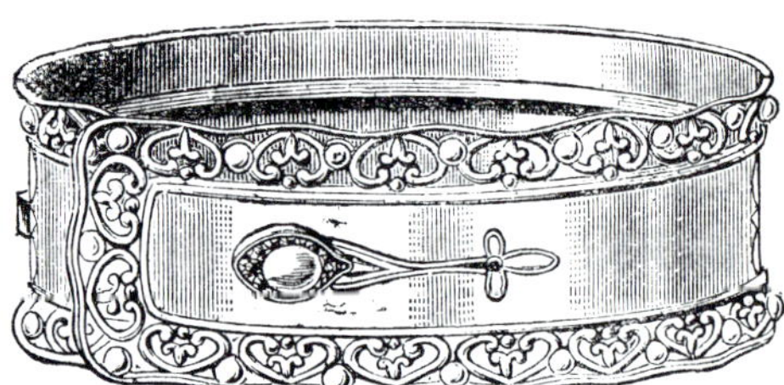

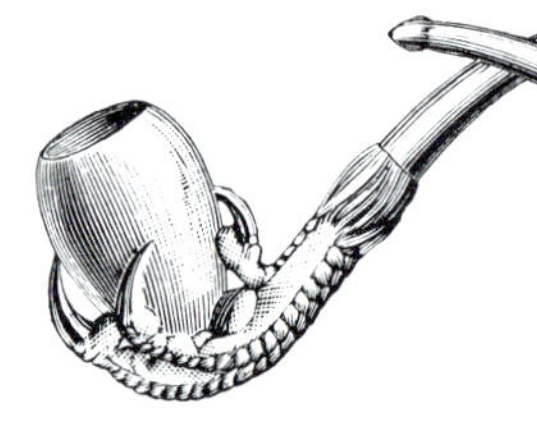

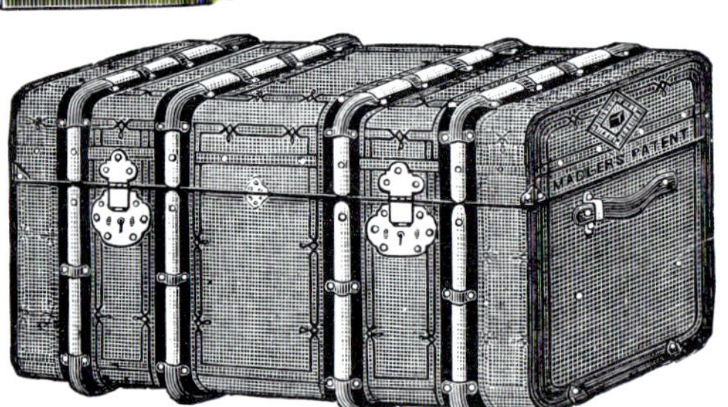

MAPPIN & WEBB
LONDON & SHEFFIELD
ANTIQUE
APPRAISALS

SINGER
VICTORIAN
CLOTHING

ANTIQUES
Butter

Antiques and Collectibles
Show and Sale
MAPPIN & WEBB
LONDON & SHEFFIELD

Antique Jewelry

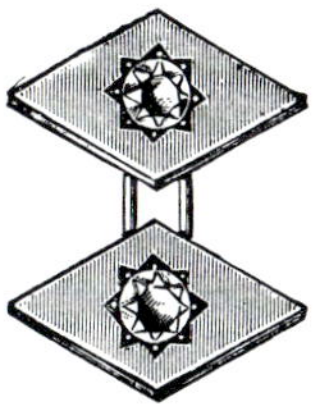

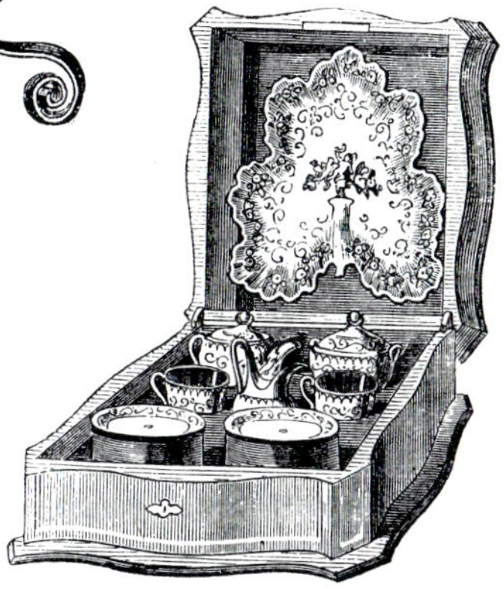

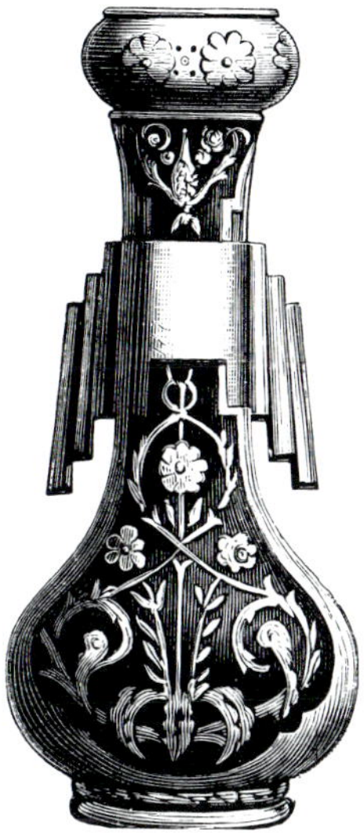

MAPPIN & WEBB
LONDON & SHEFFIELD

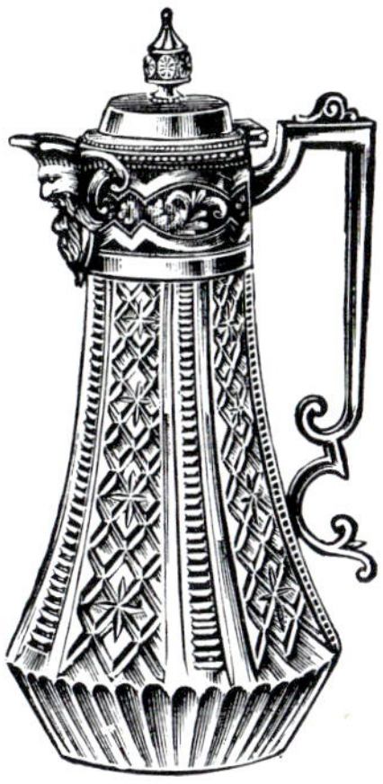

ANTIQUES FAIR

1894

ALBUM
ESTATE
AUCTION
GOLDSMITHS & SILVERSMITHS Co
112 REGENT ST. W.

ANTIQUES
ANTIQUES
MARKETPLACE
APPRAISALS
MAPPIN & WEBB
LONDON & SHEFFIELD

DEPRESSION GLASS

FLEA MARKET
TAG SALE

Antiques

Ephemera

SQUASHVILLE
COUNTY
FAIR
A READING GAME
PARKER BROTHERS, INCORPORATED
UNION
BANK
ANTIQUES
AND
FLEA
MARKET

ANTIQUES & COLLECTIBLES

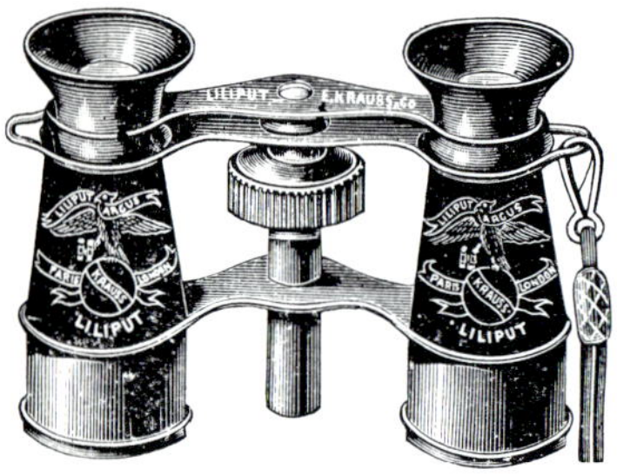

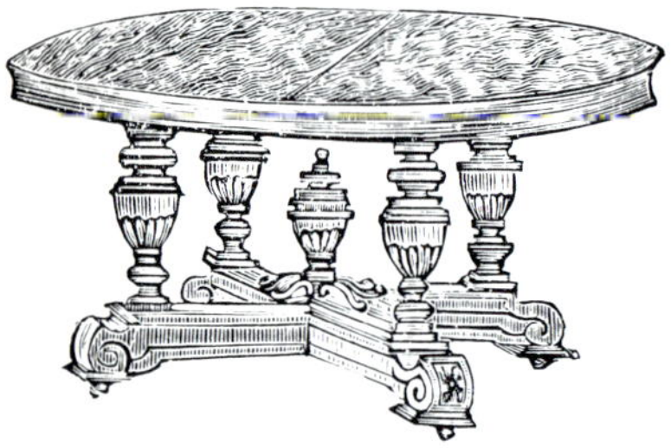

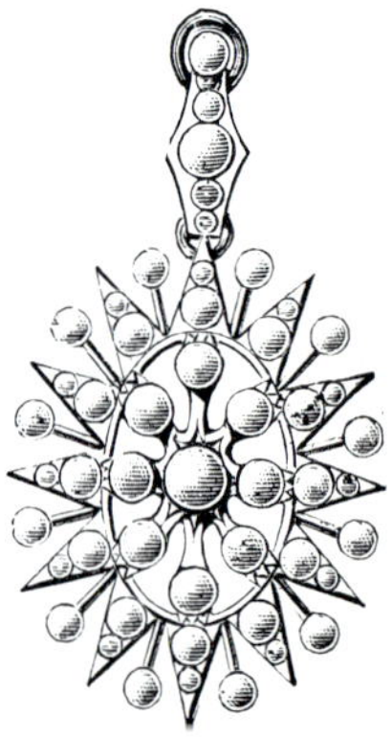

Remington
Remington Standard Typewriter No 7
WE
BUY
AND
SELL

ANTIQUES SHOW
Clocks
Dolls
Toys
Books
Cut Glass
Jewelry • Victorian Clothing

Vintage
Clothing
SCRAP
BOOK

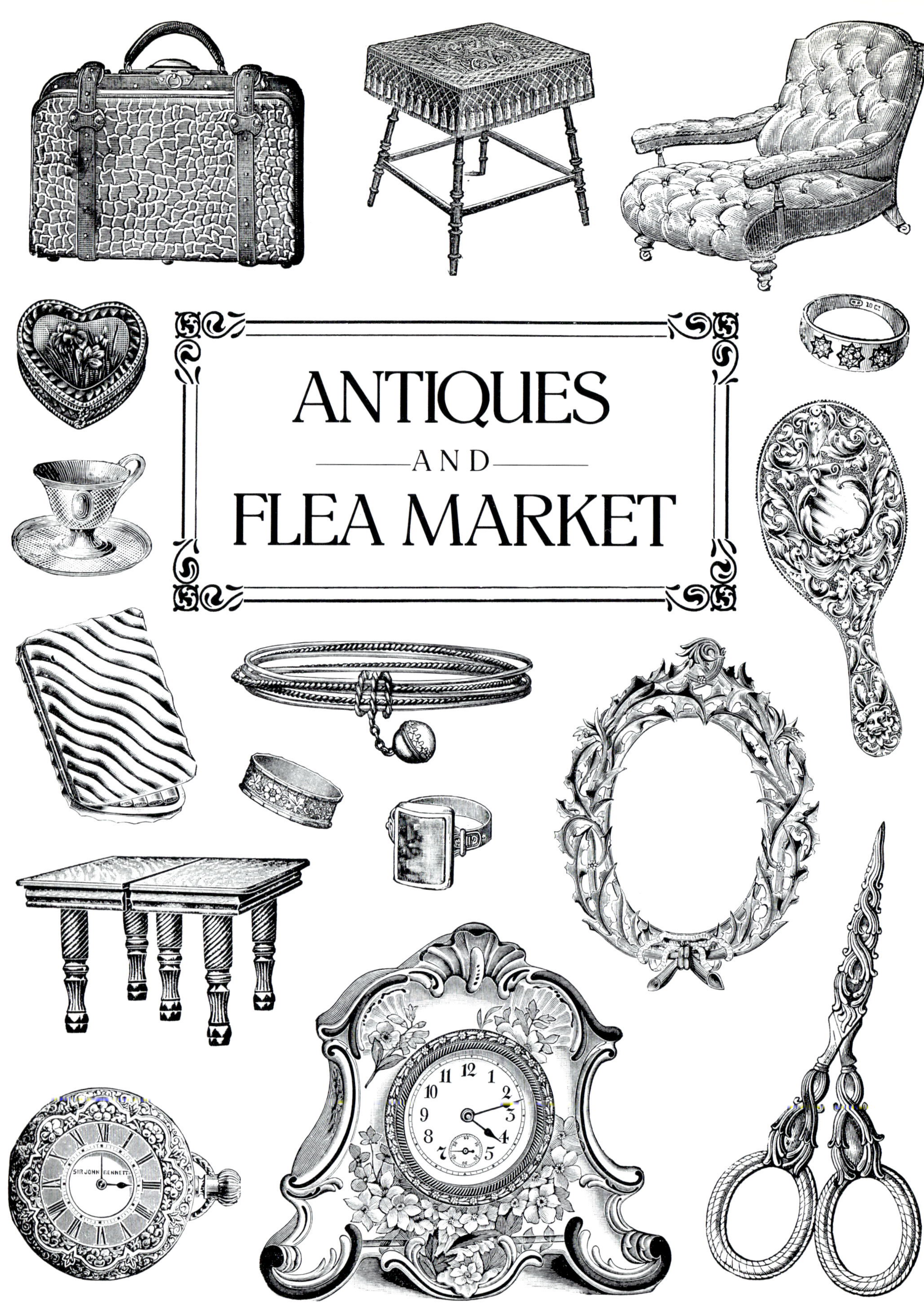
ANTIQUES
AND
FLEA MARKET
SIR JOHN BENNETT

ANTIQUES
AUCTION
Auction Gallery

ANTIQUE CLOCKS

Photographs
ANTIQUE
ORIENTAL
CARPETS

MAPPIN & WEBB
LONDON & SHEFFIELD
Antiques
Market

BARN SALE
ANTIQUE
DOLLS
and
ANTIQUE
TOYS

ANTIQUE FURNITURE

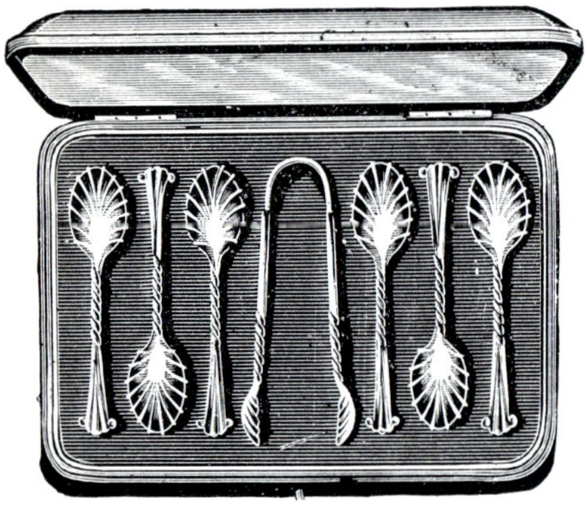

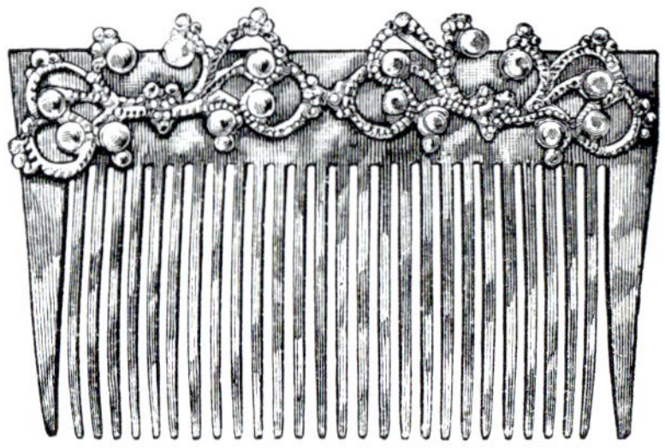

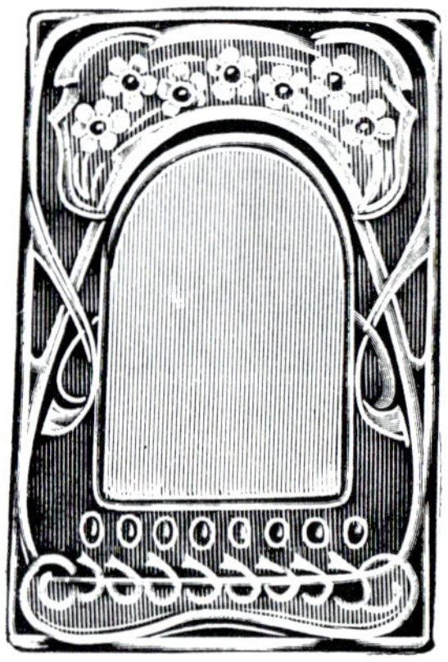

ANTIQUARIAN
BOOKS
MAPPIN & WEBB
LONDON & SHEFFIELD

MAPPIN & WEBB
LONDON & SHEFFIELD
ANTIQUES
and
COLLECTIBLES
SHOW
and
SALE

CONSIGNMENT SHOP
ANTIQUES
CENTER
VENDUE
this Day

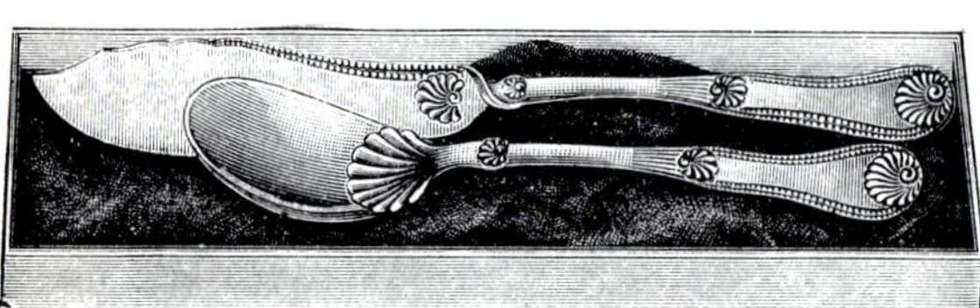

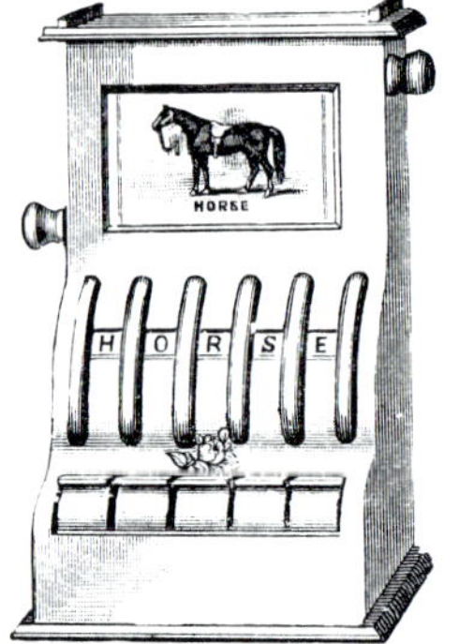

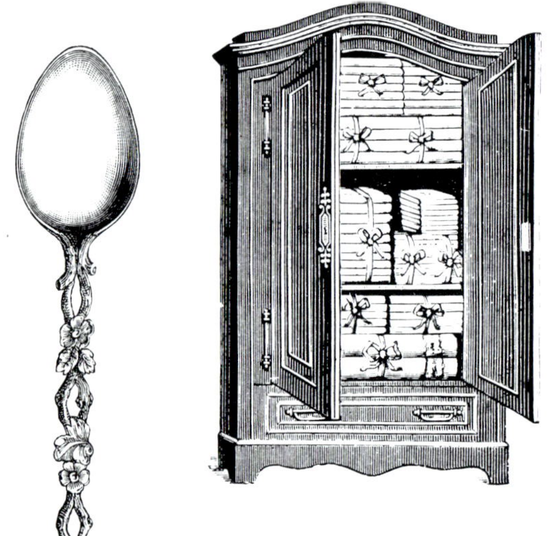

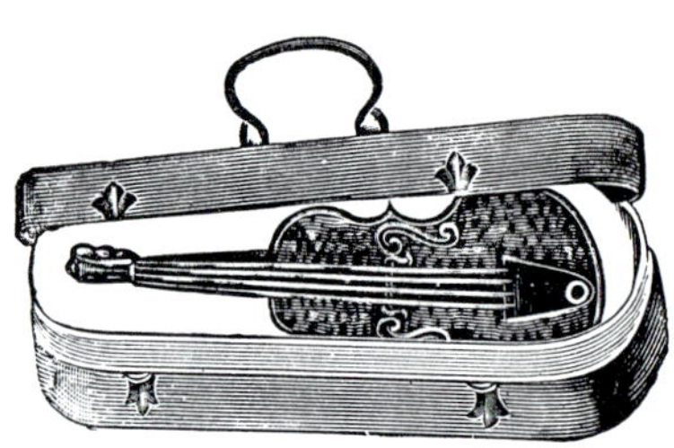

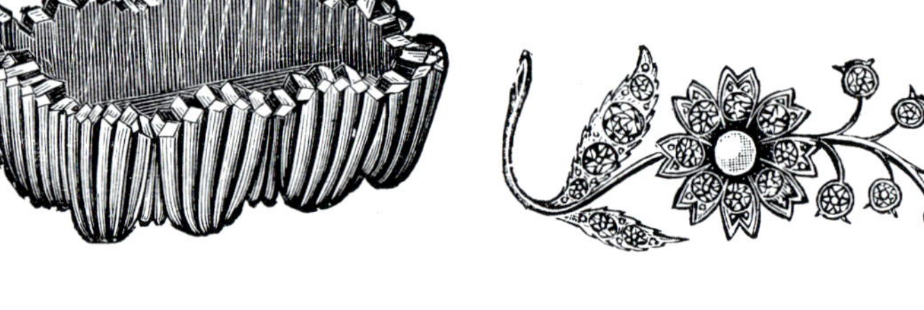

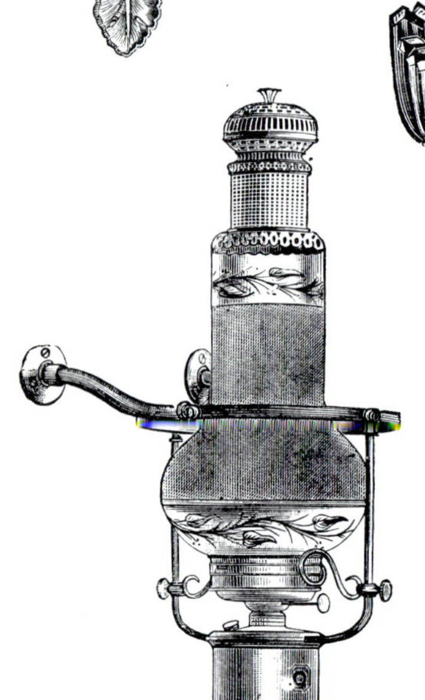

GARAGE
SALE